AMPLIFY YOUR

SUPERPOWER

A Revelation of Gifts and Talents for
Navigating Life

Amplify Your Superpower © 2023

All rights reserved.

ISBN 979-8-9875656-1-2

Superpower Guide

Your talent is God's gift to you.

What you do with it is your gift back to God.

Leo Buscaglia

Introduction: Superpower Wings
By JC Gardner

When you hear the term, "Superpower," it sounds like something related to fantasy land or maybe even animated figures, like people leaping tall buildings in a single bound or flying through the sky. Such beings may even be able to read your thoughts using magic and mind tricks or move objects without any physical touch.

If we want to bring it down to earth (pun intended), then those who are into weighting could be deemed as having superpowers, along with boxers, martial artists, and Olympians. Some countries are called "Superpowers" because of their immense wealth and status.

Having a Superpower tends to mean something uncommon, unique, unusual and to sum it up, extraordinary. And when we say something is **extraordinary**, we usually do not think of ourselves. It seems too much of a stretch to say we are special and that could be the result of many things, such as our upbringing, low self-esteem, labeling, and a host of other adjectives thrown our way.

But guess what? You are not only extraordinary, **you are beautifully and wonderfully made by the Master's hand, created in His image**. There is no one like you! He broke the mold when He designed you. No one can do what you do. Your history and journey in this life is a style all its own and cannot be replicated or duplicated, other than by your own shadow! What you've lived through, overcome, triumphed, and achieved is a solo act. The way you did it is a masterclass on its own, as there are life lessons only you can teach.

Those life lessons are your superpowers. Allow that to marinate a bit. For some of us, we have gifts and talents that are obvious, as things come easy to us: writing, singing, sewing, designing, cooking, managing and so much more. Then there are other things that may not be so obvious but clearly, they are our superpowers:

✓ You are always the one who organizes events

✓ If someone needs a prayer warrior, they call you

✓ You are always volunteering, in service to others

✓ Seeing and executing the dream comes easy to you

✓ In the midst of calm, you are the equalizer

A-hem!! (Clearing my throat.) If you are that person that is on speed-dial for one thing or another, then you better believe you have that particular superpower and probably more than one. You just need to shift your mindset into believing and claiming that which God has planted within you. You are a major link (not kink) in the chain, and you need to understand that your connectedness is divinely orchestrated.

On the following pages are 7 testimonies from women about their superpowers, and you will see that no two are the same, yet the commonality is they are women of faith, committed and dedicated to living life out loud and not squandering the gifts and talents God gave them.

Did these women always have this confidence and belief? Not at all. Listen, this life is a journey and a process. Along the way, we grow in our faith, and we expand our circle to be with others who are there to uplift, encourage, and push us to the next level so that we can boldly embrace what God has destined for us unapologetically.

After each chapter, you will find reflection questions to help you unearth your own abilities which will enable you to soar on wings like eagles. Imagine how good it will feel to know that you are using your superpowers in your home, community, workplace, business, place of worship, and so on.

Get your C.A.P.E. and fly!

C – **Confidence**: Walk in confidence that you are divinely blessed with   abilities selected just for you.

A - **Affirmations**: Say daily affirmations and keep an active prayer life.

P - **Perseverance**: Do not give up! Remember who you are and who you belong to.

E - **Encouraged**: Be encouraged! He will never leave you nor forsake you; there will be bumps along the way, but joy comes in the morning.

*Each of you should use whatever gi4 you have received to serve others, as faithful stewards of God's grace in its various forms. **1 Peter 4:10** (NIV)*

THE POWER OF FAITH
By Christelle Lilliane

Faith has been my superpower, enabling me to navigate some of the toughest times with resilience and strength. For me, faith is not only a religious belief but a way of life. It is the belief that things will work out, even when it seems impossible, and that there is a divine power guiding and supporting us through life, even in times of great difficulty and uncertainty. In this essay, I will share what I have learned about faith from my personal experiences, and how it can empower and inspire us to overcome obstacles and achieve our dreams.

My perspective on faith is that it's about taking the next step, even when one can't see what lies ahead. Faith means trusting that things will work out, even when it seems impossible. I have faced many challenges in my life, but I have always relied on my faith to overcome them.

For me, faith is not just a religious belief, but a way of life. I have found that when I am faced with difficult situations, talking to God brings me a sense of peace and comfort. This is not to say that my faith has made my life easy; I have also faced many obstacles and difficulties. However, I found that by holding on to my faith, I have been able to persevere through even the toughest times.

The phrase "walk by faith not by sight" is my own guiding principle. It means I trust in God's plan, even when I can't see what's ahead. This can be difficult at times, but I have learned to have faith that things will work out in the end. I do believe that this is the key to overcoming any obstacle.

My journey is a testament to the power of faith as I have faced many challenges, but with my unwavering faith, this has carried me through. I believe that by having faith and trusting in God's plan, anyone can overcome their struggles. This may not always be easy, but I encourage everyone to take the next step, even when you can't see what's ahead. By walking by faith, you too can find peace and satisfaction, even in the midst of difficult times.

On the following pages, I am going to share what I have learned so far from my personal experiences!

1. Have Faith in God

The loss of my beloved mother in 2011, followed by my father's passing eight years later, completely transformed my life. However, my unwavering faith in God gave me the strength and resilience to endure these trying times and use my experience to help others. Instead of letting my grief consume me, I chose to channel it into a force for good, and I am grateful for the opportunity to make a positive impact in the lives of those around me. Faith in God has been my source of comfort, inspiration, and guidance countless times throughout my life. It is the belief that there is a divine power or force that guides and supports us through life, even in times of great difficulty and uncertainty.

My faith in God has also become my source of strength and comfort in times of crisis. When people are faced with illness, loss, or other challenges, many people turn to God for guidance and support. I am a 17-year cancer survivor, having been diagnosed with Stage 4 stomach cancer when my baby boy was just three years-old and my daughter was only eleven months old. During my time at the cancer center, my husband had to step up and take on the roles of both a father and a mother to our two young children. I attribute my survival and perseverance to my faith in God, which kept me going throughout my battle with Stage 4 stomach cancer. With God's help, I was able to overcome the illness, and I am grateful for every day of life that I have been given since then. The belief that there is a divine being with endless power watching over us can be a source of hope and resilience, even in the darkest of times. Do you believe it?

My faith in God remains an essential aspect of my life. It provided me with a sense of purpose, meaning, and connection to something greater than ourselves. It helped me navigate the challenges of life and find a deeper sense of peace and fulfillment. Ultimately, it is undeniable that my faith in God brought me the power to inspire and guide people through their life challenges.

2. Anything Is Possible with Faith

Faith is a powerful force that can change the world. When we have faith in God, we believe that anything is possible. We know that there is a divine higher power at work and that we are never alone. This belief can give us the strength and courage to pursue our dreams and overcome any obstacle that comes our way. Faith is something where you believe that whatever obstacles come your way, you know that you will get what you are praying for, you see and understand that everything that is happening are just trials that make you stronger and get you ready for where you should be.

Faith is believing in the promises of God even when you haven't seen them!

3. Miracles In My Life Because of Faith

Many people have experienced miraculous events in their lives because of their faith in God. These miracles can range from small acts of kindness to major life changes. For example, some people have overcome serious illnesses or found the courage to face their fears because of their faith in God.

Faith is a very strong Emotion! It is a powerful tool that can help us to live our best lives.

It gives us hope, courage, and the strength to overcome obstacles. When we have faith, we know that anything is possible and that the impossible can become possible through the power of the divine. By experiencing faith, we can experience the love and compassion of God in our lives and find meaning and purpose in our existence.

4. Faith Provides Hope

Faith in God can provide us with a sense of hope and peace, even in the face of adversity. It helps us to see the world in a positive light and to believe that everything will work out for the best. Faith gives people the courage to keep going despite life's challenges because we believe that there is a divine being watching over us and guiding us to what is best for all of us. Many of us are born to believe that everything happens for a reason and that nothing will ever know what's best for us but the one true God.

5. Strengthens Our Resolve

When we have faith, we are more likely to persevere in the face of adversity. Our faith gives us the strength and courage to keep going, even when things are difficult. It is because we believe that difficult times keep us strong and that everything happens for a reason. We believe that if we focus on our goals, with ease and calm because we have faith that through hard work, the divine power will give us what we are worthy of.

6. Fosters a Positive Attitude

Faith can help us to develop a positive and optimistic outlook on life. It allows us to focus on the good things in life and to be grateful for what we have. Faith provides us with a powerful inner strength and calmness that helps us to overcome challenges, stand up for mistakes, and move forward.

7. Enhances Our Relationships

Faith can help us to build stronger relationships with others. It teaches us to be kind, compassionate, and forgiving, which are important qualities for building strong and meaningful relationships. You see, anything is possible with faith. It is because you have a strong and positive aura that all things will be well, even relationships with family and co-workers.

8. Brings Purpose to Our Lives

Faith can provide us with a sense of purpose and meaning. It helps us to see our lives in a broader context and to understand why we are here. When you have faith, you find reasons to keep going and to have a positive attitude toward things. You can decide clearly with an open mind because you are properly positioned in a way that life goes on and you are positioned to get up and take action.

9. Offers a Source of Comfort

Faith can provide us with comfort and peace in times of distress. It reminds us that there is a higher power at work and that we are never truly alone. It can also bring solace in times of trouble by reminding us of our connection to something greater than ourselves. It provides hope that our struggles have purpose and meaning and that we are not alone in facing them. Believing in a higher power can help us find comfort and peace, even in the midst of distress.

10. Inspires Us to Help Others

Faith often inspires us to reach out and help others. By serving others, we can experience the love and compassion of God in our lives and make a positive difference in the world. Helping others can give us a sense of purpose and fulfillment and can bring hope and healing to those in need. Through acts of service, we can make a positive impact on the world and share the goodness of our faith.

A few years ago, I visited my friend, Yvonne, who owns an international shipping franchise. During our conversation, she expressed her intention to close the store due to outstanding debts owed to her landlord. I reassured her that God would make a way and we prayed about it before I left.

Two months later, the COVID-19 pandemic occurred, and her landlord could not evict her due to a court order. Yvonne has since remained open and is grateful for the faith that helped her through the tough times.

On a personal note, as the firstborn of seven siblings, I am a role model for my brothers and sisters. Because I prioritize faith over fear, they often seek my guidance and follow my example when making decisions.

11. Promotes Inner Peace

Faith can help us to find inner peace and tranquility. It allows us to let go of worries and fears and to focus on the present moment. It provides a grounding that helps us release anxieties and fears to live in the present with greater mindfulness and gratitude. Through faith, we can cultivate a deeper sense of inner tranquility and serenity.

12. Encourages Personal Growth

Faith can inspire us to grow and develop as individuals. It helps us recognize our strengths and weaknesses so we can work on becoming our best versions. Faith gives us the courage to work on areas that need improvement. Through faith, we can learn important life lessons, develop new skills, and foster a sense of purpose that fuels our growth and development.

13. Leads to a Fulfilling Life

When we have faith, we are more likely to lead fulfilling and meaningful lives. Our faith helps us to see the beauty in the world and to live each day to the fullest. It helps us appreciate the goodness in the world and to find purpose and direction in our daily lives.

In a nutshell, faith has the power to transform our lives in countless ways. It provides us with hope, strength, and purpose, and helps us to build stronger relationships and to lead more fulfilling lives. By embracing faith, you can experience the love and compassion of God in your lives, grounded in service and gratitude, and find meaning and purpose in your existence.

Reflection/Notes

What are your key takeaways?

Were there any surprising moments that spoke to your soul?

What would you share with others?

What superpowers aligned with yours?

About Christelle Lilliane

Christelle Lilliane is a successful businesswoman and author who was born in Cotonou, Benin, West Africa, and has been living in Illinois for the past 25 years. She has a strong family background and has excelled in multiple businesses. Her strong personality was inherited from her father, a colonel in the army who always expected excellence from her. On the other hand, her mother instilled in her the importance of kindness, which has become a core value in Christelle's life. She has consistently excelled in every field of life and is a perfect example of how one can fight their problems while still thriving.

Christelle has been in the beauty industry for over 15 years and owns her own beauty salon. She has also been doing event planning for the last 10 years and has been in the export/import business for the past 11 years, dealing with customs. She is a great communicator and is using her skills to empower youth, women, and men of all ages and backgrounds worldwide. Her upcoming book, "Change Your Focus. Change Your Life" is aimed at helping people overcome adversity and become the best version of themselves.

Christelle has a wealth of experience, having been a Mary Kay cosmetics sales director and a Mary Kay car driver. She has received multiple Mary Kay awards, diamond rings, Mary Kay vacation vouchers, and much more. She is also a cancer survivor, has been with her husband for over 20 years, and is a mother of two teenagers.

Connect with Christelle Lilliane:

Facebook: https://www.facebook.com/Christellelillianeauthor

Website: christellelilliane.com

Email: contact@christellelilliane.com

Making the Crooked Paths Straight: The Gift of Organization
By Madonna Williams

This gift of organization is most memorable for me at the age of 10 years old. As I stood on the green, pink, and white animal print laminate floors with the crisp air blowing though the kitchen window, there I was, arranging momma's kitchen cabinets. This was such an exciting time for me. Putting all the canned corn on one row, then the green beans, sweet peas and whatever else momma had in those cabinets. I would even rearrange the refrigerator from time to time.

Fast forward twenty years as a bookkeeper at a metropolitan public school, I had more opportunities to do the thing I love...Organizing.

Not only was I able to put money together, books, supplies, meetings, etc., but I found that I had a great way of helping teachers get a lot of things organized.

I arrived two hours before student arrivals to prepare the necessary paperwork for the principal but what I found each day was a teacher or two -- or five -- or eight -- standing in my doorway with an issue they needed to be resolved.

On one occasion, I would help them plan out a school event/field trip; on another occasion, I helped plan out their personal budget or create a timeline to maximize a strategy for them to complete their master's program. People were coming to me constantly for work related, family, and personal issues.

It was during this same season of time that I had an inner growth spurt. So while I was organizing everyone else's life, my inner-self and my personal life was disorganized to the point I was no longer thriving; I was actually dying a death of low morale, low energy, and just not wanting to be present. As a woman of faith, the scripture came to me: "Your husband will wash you with the water of the Word." I took that very literal, but it was God saying the *Spirit-man* was going to water me and wash me in the Word, and understanding this different interpretation, I began to allow myself to be watered in a different way. I always attributed the watering was coming from my spouse and wondered over and over again why I was not being "fed," but once I realized it was God doing the watering, that meant my resources were endless.

To help me redefine my mindset, though, I needed to access *different resources*. I was led to read four different motivational books a day, mostly in the morning. My reading list was something like:

- "How to Win Friends And Influence People," by Dale Carnegie.
- Scientific audiobooks or video on Youtube like: "Cleaning Up Your Mental Mess," by Dr. Caroline Leaf.
- Driving home, I would listen to a CD like: "Crucial Conversations," by Patterson, Grenny, McMillian, and Switzler.
- And I would end the day reading something like: "The Magic of Thinking BIG," by David J. Schwartz.

Before this season, I wasn't interested in reading at all, save the occasional scriptural reading and deep studies of the Hebrew and Greek translations on the weekend.

But reading these kinds of books, it was as if I finally found someone who spoke my language, who was speaking life to me at a time in my life when I was searching for answers. I literally remember asking God, "Why hasn't someone told me this stuff and where are the people who can teach me what I need to grow?"

If you've ever asked God a question, you should know that He will come through with the answer to every problem for every situation.

You can't put new wine into old wineskins. If you think about organization, you have to declutter that which no longer serves you. These books opened my eyes to a different way of not only working on the external aspects of life but rearranging my mental space.

Reading so many books in a short period of time caused my whole world to shift which led me to reach out to my pastor for spiritual guidance.

At that time, I had felt that I had grown inwardly and the walls that used to keep me bound were now released. As scary and as freeing that turned out to be, for me, my marriage was the basis for this conversation with spiritual help.

However, what I was seeking was now seeking me; I thought that when I sat in my pastor's beautiful study that he uses for counseling sessions that he was going to give me wisdom for marriage. Through our conversations and with spiritual enlightenment, what he actually gave me was a key to a whole new world. This key has allowed me to use my organizational skills in vastly different ways that I didn't even realize was possible for me.

Let's understand that organization comes in different forms. It's not just putting things in order. It can be applied to things that happen in your everyday life: How do you manage your expectations? How do you advance your career?

When you walk in your home or your office, how do you want it to look and feel?

And then reflecting on your internal "storage," if you wake up chaotic, depressed, unhappy, thoughts all over the place, it can hinder many areas of your life without you even knowing it.

For me, out of fear, I was hoarding a lot of junk out of what was considered custom, old-school expectations, and it was blocking my purpose. Once I released the mental clutter, it allowed me to flourish and move into other spaces I thought were not for me.

In releasing those deep-rooted limitations, I was able to venture into starting my own podcast with no experience, writing books that I always told God

I could not write, creating a YouTube channel, and I had the courage to travel to Spain for one month solo to use my gift of singing, just to name a few.

During my awakening sessions with my Pastor, there was a realization that all of my gifts, talents, and time were going into my children. I was there for them and for others, nurturing, mentoring, providing practical advice and more. He had a vision of me moving into the Life Coach space. When he presented me with this seed, I had no idea of its potential and honestly, I didn't know what a coach was or that it was actually a thing.

Although I have been in the presence of a person who had coached, they were presented to me as a speaker, so I had no idea all of the facets related to being a coach and how many of them neatly fit into my personality and character traits.

This was an open door for me to have a different kind creative outlet. The benefit for me positioning myself this way was I got to show others and help them understand there is greatness on the inside of them screaming to come out and be all the things we are meant to be. It gives me immense joy is to see the scales fall off their faces as they gain clearer vision for their life. They get clarity, confidence, and an expansion of themselves. They are able to do more than they thought. Some of the nuggets I've imparted along the way are:

- It's safe for you to say you desire something else.
- It's safe to move away from tradition.

- It's safe to call the truck to come pick up all of the things that no longer serve you and reorganize your life so that you can walk in the purpose that God has for you.

Remember, you have already been given a gift of something so extraordinary that only you possess. My question is, "Have you watered it?" It's easy to look at someone else and think that their gift is better, bigger, or more influential than the one you received but here's the thing: you have to work it.

Your gift can't grow itself.

So, I would encourage you to keep growing in the areas that bring you joy, excitement and inspiration. You may be saying *but MaDonna, I don't know what brings me joy...* and I can understand that you've been on a rollercoaster just doing the same thing day in and day out. But stretch yourself; make a date with yourself to do something different each week. Take some time to meditate and do some soul searching for what you believe would make you happy. What would cause you to say, "I'm living my best life?" Do something that you know you will look forward to doing. I want you to go to your calendar right now and schedule an activity for you to do that's different from what you normally do on a weekly/monthly basis. These different activities of intentional discernment will help to re-ignite the gift(s) that may be lying dormant.

Just know an organized life will open doors and give you some of the answers you are looking for which are also looking for you.

Reflection/Notes

What are your key takeaways?

Were there any surprising moments that spoke to your soul?

What would you share with others?

What superpowers aligned with yours?

About MaDonna Williams

MaDonna Williams is a passionate mindset coach who supports impact driven professional women by guiding them to create their own legacies for the future. Through a consultative process, MaDonna gives her clients a unique, tailored approach designed to help women overcome their resistance of achieving greatness. Her tools and techniques transform your mindset from moving out of the shadows to being seen and heard through podcasts, YouTube channels, authorship, and speaking on stages, to name a few.

After years of supporting others (including her four children), a breast cancer diagnosis reminded her of her grandmothers' words: "Don't just exist. LIVE!" MaDonna's personal journey of self-rediscovery and living commenced in answering a spiritual calling to become a certified mindset coach so she could help restore and empower women on their journey to self-worth, wholeness, and becoming fearless.

In addition to her mindset coaching business, MaDonna is an international singer, published author, inspirational speaker and loves to garden while being assisted by her sidekick cat named Shadow. She also works in the school district, which her organizational gifts and talents serve many.

Join her free Facebook Group called (Ignite Your Confidence) to get the tools you need to build the six-figure empire of your dreams.

Connect with MaDonna:

Free 30 Minute Breakthrough Call -
https://bit.ly/Speak_with_MaDonna

Facebook Group – Ignite Your Confidence
https://sites.google.com/view/igniteyour-confidence/home

Facebook Business Page – MaDonna INcourage

YouTube- MaDonna INcourage

Instagram – MaDonna INcourage

LinkedIn – MaDonna INcourage

CAN YOU SEE IT?
By Deborah Franklin

Can you see it? Can you see it? You don't see the room packed on different continents filled with women who want to hear what you have to say. Really, you don't see it? I can see it, and I'm expecting it. When your superpower is being a visionary, you see it before everyone else does and the folk around you are looking at you like you're one step from the padded cell. Yes, this superpower can be a gift and a curse. As a visionary, we see the big picture, the end results, the stage, and my name in lights on the marquee. We also see the people. We see the products, but we sometimes don't see what it takes to meet the end results, but we welcome the challenge.

Being a visionary is a quality that sets individuals apart from the rest. It is the ability to see beyond what is immediately visible, to perceive what is possible and to work towards making it a reality. Visionaries are those who have the courage to dream big, and the determination to make those dreams a reality. One of my big dreams was to do missions in Africa.

While in college I went on my first mission trip to Zimbabwe, and I was hooked. I knew that missions were my calling, but I didn't know how I was going to accomplish it. I kept living and every step in my walk led to missions. It was my deciding factor to become an ordained minister and to continue to work with children. Fast forward to 2021. I was set to do my first mission trip to Lagos, Nigeria. Ok, yes that was at the end of the pandemic and information was shaky. I just knew this was going to be the launch of something big. Little did I know God had different plans.

I made it all the way to Lagos to be deported. Yes, I said I was deported because I didn't have a visa. I was like, *God I know what you showed me.* You gave me the finances and the supplies to get here. I made it through all the checkpoints, but now I can't get in. I like to call this my Moses moment. I heard clearly that day this is not the place for you. You will see the promised land, but this is not where you are supposed to enter. One good thing is that I had partnered with a Church Girl CEO there, and she was allowed to meet me and what I like to call "airport jail" and get the items for the mission giveaway. God showed me the power of pivoting. I may not have been able to get in, but the mission project was still able to happen.

Yes, I was disappointed, but I didn't let it stop me. I knew that God had something bigger for me, so I couldn't give up on the vision. I knew I was called to task. I just had to be in the right place. God then opened doors in Kenya. Real relationships were birthed. It started with giving aid to an orphanage and then an inbox from someone who was sharing her services as a social media manager. We connected, and the rest is history. We were able to partner, get the correct visas and partner with an orphanage there that we were able to send much needed supplies. We were also able to do a women's workshop in Nairobi and Kitale,

Kenya. Remember, I said God had shown me teaching on stage full of women.

Yes, I'm getting chills thinking about it. I'll be honest, never in a million years did I think I would be a real bonafide international speaker. As a visionary, we have to trust the process and not give up on what God has shown us.

Ok, think about it. What if I had just given up after being deported? What if I had questioned or doubted what I knew God had told me? I would not have been able to achieve what God had told me to do. I couldn't let setbacks slow me down or turn me around. I knew what I saw, and I was determined to achieve the goal. Was it easy? No, but it got done.

To be a visionary, one must possess several qualities. The first is imagination. Visionaries are able to create mental pictures of what could be and then work to make those pictures a reality. They have the ability to think outside the box and to see things from different angles. They are not constrained by conventional thinking and are willing to take risks in pursuit of their vision. When you have a vision, you have to operate with multiple lenses. So many times, operating outside of the box feels like you are alone, but you still have to trust what God showed you. The second quality that a visionary must possess is creativity. Visionaries are able to create new and innovative ideas, products, or services. They are not content with the status quo and are always looking for ways to improve upon what already exists. They are able to connect seemingly disparate ideas to create something new and exciting. I continually pray God will activate the creativity I need to successfully accomplish this goal.

Another important quality that a visionary must possess is the ability to communicate their vision effectively. This involves not only being able to articulate their ideas clearly, but also being able to inspire others to believe in their vision. Visionaries must be able to paint a picture of what the future could be like and then convince others to help them make it a reality. Remember, God is not the author of confusion; therefore, when it is time to share the vision, the people who He needs to hear it will heed the call and help you to make it come to pass. Don't get caught up on the ones who don't support your vision.

One of the most important qualities that a visionary must possess is persistence. Bringing a vision to life requires a tremendous amount of hard work and determination and building a team. Building a team that can see your vision is hard, but it can be done. As a visionary, it is hard to trust because you have to share your vision with others to make it a reality. Yes, trust is hard, but that's called trusting in God to send you the team that can carry the weight of the vision. Now, this is not easy, but it will happen.

I knew I needed a team, but I didn't know where to find them. Trust me, God will surprise you where your team will come from. Honestly, my team was not who I thought they would be. My team is international. My assistant is in Kenya and board members are in various states. My team also includes members from all different walks of life and industries that did not fit my vision. I just knew I would be having board meetings in the office and have the ability to do activities at the drop of a dime, but God saw different. Now my team flies in for meetings and fusses at me when I don't depend on them. Depending on others is definitely something I struggle with because for so long, it was just me. I did what I had to do to make the vision happen. But, when I looked back, that was something I had to do to show my future team that I was serious about the vision God showed me. All I kept hearing James 2:17 (NKJV) 17: *Thus also faith by itself, if it does not have works, is dead.* I had to operate in the faith that I saw that it was going to come to fruition. I had to put the work in and believe in the dream no matter what was happening around me.

There was an event I was planning, and I had big plans for the event. I asked people to help me, but they didn't show up for me. I had an agenda that I shared, but no one followed it. I could have been discouraged but I wasn't. Now don't get me wrong I was disappointed, but God showed me clear as day they were not supposed to be on my team, and they could not handle the weight of the vision that God had given me. When you have a **big vision**, you have to trust that God will give you **provision**. One rule that I have learned over the years is that if the vision God gives you doesn't give you fear or is something you can just go to the bank and make happen, that vision is not big enough. Get ready for the stretching. If you are reading this, I already know this section has resonated with you in a way that has you wondering if she is sitting next to me or has been listening to my calls or text messages. Get ready for the overflow and operate in more than enough.

Another key to forming a successful team is that they need to see your vision, but they cannot be 'yes' people. 'Yes' people make you feel good, but they are not good for you. Build your team with persons with different skill sets. For example, you need to have someone who is the facts and figures person. They help the visionary stay straight. In my experience, this person doesn't change the vision but assists in giving the vision form. I'm the type that if I see it, I'm ready to do it, no matter what the cost or obstacles I have to jump over. Visionaries must be willing to overcome obstacles and setbacks along the way and to keep pushing forward even when the going gets tough. Having to make pivots is real. One has to accept that God does show the end results, but the journey is unnavigated. Think about it from the perspective of tying your shoe. Your mother may have taught you one way, but your friends taught you another. Doesn't mean that either way is right or wrong, but your shoe was tied. As a visionary, don't get caught up in having to start over or having to adjust what has to be done to finish.

One of the biggest challenges that visionaries face is skepticism. When someone comes up with a new and innovative idea, it is often met with skepticism from those who are comfortable with the status quo. Visionaries must be able to overcome this skepticism and to convince others to believe in their vision. You cannot give up because the support you seek doesn't come from the expected circle. Don't let that discourage you. Remember, everyone is not going to share or see your vision. **This is why you're the visionary**.

Another challenge that visionaries face is the fear of failure. Bringing a vision to life requires taking risks, and there is always the possibility that things will not work out as planned. Visionaries must be able to overcome this fear and to keep pushing forward, even when the road ahead seems uncertain. But what sets a visionary apart from the average person is that fear doesn't paralyze you. Fear doesn't make you be quiet in rooms that you know you deserve to be in. Fear, for visionaries, is what motivates us. Yes, we may have to self-positive talk into overdrive, but this is the fuel we need to quiet the noise of fear.

In conclusion, being a visionary is not an easy task. It requires a combination of imagination, creativity, communication, persistence, and courage. Being a visionary is a rare and powerful gift that has the potential to change the world. Visionaries are the ones who see the future before it arrives, who imagine new possibilities and bring them to life through their creativity, purpose, and conviction. They are the leaders who inspire others to join them in pursuit of a better future, and their impact on society is immeasurable. You have been chosen and destined for this calling. God chose you. Now show up and trust the process.

Reflection/Notes

What are your key takeaways?

Were there any surprising moments that spoke to your soul?

What would you share with others?

What superpowers aligned with yours?

About Deborah Franklin

Deborah is the Founder/CEO of Conversations Entertainment Group that is the corporate headquarters for Deborah Franklin Publishing and Church Girl CEO. With over 20 years in the entertainment and education industry, she has the knowledge and expertise to assist you to catapult your career to the next level.

Deborah Franklin also has a heart for women to expand their mindsets past what they can see and she encourages them to not be afraid to tell their stories to the world. As a survivor of verbal abuse, she has learned to rise above what has been said to her and about her to be the authentic representative of who she was created to be.

Deborah Franklin is the author of 'adjectives,' '21 Days 21 Minutes of Prayer & Meditation,' '#5 30 Days of Motivation & Inspiration' and 'The Prayer of Jabez in the Marketplace'. She is host of Conversations w/Deborah Franklin and has been working as a media coach for several years with clients who are authors, speakers, and entertainers.

Deborah also uses her platform to give other aspiring artists an outlet to let their talents shine. Her ultimate goal in life is to help others ignite the power within to propel them to their destiny.

Connect with Deborah Franklin:

Website: www.churchgirlceo.org

Email: info@churchgirlceo.org

Cell: 443.454.3751

A Fair Prayer
By Amy Philpott

It was Friday morning, and I was busy setting up my jewelry booth at my favorite festival. Suddenly I'm embraced from behind and I hear a very familiar voice say "You're here!" I turn around and I see my sweet friend that had been doing this festival with me for ten years. However, he looked different. It was as if he was almost glowing. He must have noticed my stare. He started to tear up and was proud to tell me that he finally got clean, sober, and found Jesus. "You never judged me, Amy, and you knew all of the awful things that I had done. You always welcomed me with open arms and a friendly smile. And when you prayed for me, I knew you sincerely meant every word. I knew I had to make a change and I did."

My name is Amy Philpott and my superpower is the ability to pray with you.

I had always been sort of an introverted person, but secretly wished I could be more extroverted. Little did I know that God would bless me with this gift of prayer to make that come true. Along with this gift of prayer came a sense of calm over most situations. It didn't matter if they were my own or someone else's. It started with my family, then my friends, and now even total strangers have come to me for prayer during their challenging times. I've been told that I have this big picture vision and can see around and through the overwhelm, bringing hope and a calming peace.

At the same festival several years prior, a woman walked into my very crowded booth during the headlining musical act of the evening. She looked distraught and I felt Holy Spirit tugging at my heart. I asked her if there was anything in particular she needed. She responded that she was just looking at the jewelry.

"Can I pray with you?" I asked in return. She began to cry and grabbed my hands and together, we began to pray. Others around us joined in by laying hands on us as we prayed together. But, that...that isn't even the best part! The headlining act stopped singing mid-song and signaled her band to cut the music. She could see into my booth and proceeded to tell the crowd that something amazing was going on. They started a new song, "It is Well, With My Soul". The audience of nearly 1,000 soon joined her in song as did other vendors and those who were just passing by. More joined us in prayer as we could feel the weight of their hands on us. Holy Spirit came and this woman's burdens were lifted by the end of the song. She said she had never felt such peace. In all honesty, I hadn't either. There wasn't a dry eye anywhere. The selfless act of the performer saw an opportunity to be the hands and feet of Jesus for a stranger; she led so many others to do the same. The love of a community for one woman was overflowing.

And it started with "Can I pray with you?" That night will never be forgotten.

Last year, at the same festival, on Saturday, I witnessed and experienced something that to this day, I have no words to describe, but I will do my best. My mom, sister, and I heard the helicopter coming. The emergency life services team was doing their annual display for the community. We went to our respected places to hold down displays as the wind from the helicopter would kick up enough momentum to knock a few loose items over. What happened next was truly unexpected and downright terrifying. The pilot apparently misjudged his descent and flew too close to the vendors and landed entirely too close to me. All of my hanging displays were blowing back and forth like the pirate ship ride at an amusement park; busts flew off almost like cannon shots and my spinning displays were twirling faster than fan blades with jewelry flying off in machine-gun style fashion. Dirt was flying everywhere.

Was this really happening? Clearly it was a real nightmare that I couldn't shake myself awake from. Then I heard a ripping sound and the sound of metal creaking. Skylights were ripped into my brand-new tent canopy and the frame was buckling. Had it not been anchored down to cement construction blocks, my three-tent display would have collapsed and gotten caught in the force of the aircraft's vortex and scattered everywhere.

As the chopper blades stopped spinning, all I could do was stand there in silence. *Missile marketing* wasn't exactly how I had planned on "spreading the word" about my jewelry business with my products literally flying in all directions. The only fearful thought I had was, ***it still has to leave***. In other words, when it lifted off from its location, I knew it would be a repeat as it ascended into the air, leaving a cyclone in its wake.

This whole thing was almost like an out-of-body experience. Somehow seeing the damage, I still had this overwhelming sense of peace. I couldn't change what happened, but I could do my best to change what would happen next. The three of us couldn't repair the damage or manage to hold everything down by ourselves. I called the director who came and saw the damages. She was so apologetic and just horrified. Before long, it was time for the chopper to leave. The director had sent multiple volunteers down to assist other vendors on that side of the festival, including 15 for my space. (My space was 12x36.) Even then, it was still a difficult task to complete for 18 people. The volunteers were so compassionate and couldn't believe how calm I stayed. Festival goers had been graciously returning items that flew out of the space during the event. Even the mayor came by to personally apologize and promised he would make things right.

Sunday came and my heart was heavy seeing the rips in my tent waiving at me as we started the last day of the festival. Word had gotten out pretty quickly about the helicopter incident and we found that while we had the most damage, we weren't the only ones. I remember wanting to just not talk about it anymore, not because it made me upset, but it deeply saddened my heart.

Pryor to the festival opening, several vendors came by and made several large purchases. It just seemed odd. One of my vendor friends came in, and as she was making her purchase, just smiled and said it was going to be ok. Some of the regular vendors got together and decided that they were going to come help.

After years of helping them and praying with them, it was the least they could do.

Around lunchtime, a gentleman that I recognized from years coming to the fair came down and just frowned. After we talked for a bit, he said he couldn't afford to buy a new tent for me but hoped that what he had would be enough to get most of it paid for - - all this while he reached into his wallet and pulled out cash. I couldn't stop crying, a bit in disbelief.

A familiar lady (though I couldn't place her at the time) came by and purchased over $100 worth of my children's jewelry and made nearly the same purchase amount in my women's line. As I was handing her change back to her, she refused it, hugged me and said, "It is well with my soul."

I never imagined that this gift God gave me would bring such reward. I wonder how the outcome of my personal situation would have changed had I not met it with the gift of God's grace and calm. I wonder how things would have been different had I refused to be a steward of His gift. The gift didn't manifest how I thought it would. I was simply expecting to just develop a bigger personality. Then God goes above and beyond, like the God of more than enough that He is and gives this bigger and bolder personality a purpose. It all comes back to loving Jesus and making Him known. In my line of work, I get to meet so many people. Some know Him. Some don't. So when you see me at an event, in person, or online, it might first look like it's all about the bling, but it's truly all about **THE KING**.

What has excited me the most about this heavenly gift is seeing that it has been passed down to each of our four children. They each exude compassion, love, and genuine kindness to their family, friends, and strangers. When our oldest daughter was four, she insisted on bringing her purse to the store. On our shopping trip, she would pull out a drawing and hand it to a total stranger with a hug and said she made it special just for them and that God knew she would see them that day. I've watched our kids pull their own money together to buy food for local food drives, come home jacketless because a child at the park didn't have one, and have seen them praying with their friends over real issues happening in their lives. I remember going to a semi-pro baseball game and our kids stopped and thanked and prayed with every police officer, first-responder, and veteran that they met. Our youngest just turned two and no matter where we go, she greets everyone (and I mean everyone) with the biggest smile and "Hiiiiiii. Have a great daaaaay!" that you have ever heard. Being able to also witness our three older children enter into situations that most would struggle with,

with a sense of calm, has been mind-blowing. The spiritual maturity that they have at just six, eight, and eleven is uncanny. Hearing them say, "Lets pray about it," or "Holy Spirit said..." has brought an overwhelming feeling of joy and thanksgiving to our lives.

Thank you, Lord, for this gift and the overflowing abundance of generational blessings that have come and will come from it.

Reflection/Notes

What are your key takeaways?

Were there any surprising moments that spoke to your soul?

What would you share with others?

What superpowers aligned with yours?

About Amy Philpott

Wife, mom, teacher, volunteer, prayer warrior, The Queen of Bling, all of these titles could be used to describe Amy Philpott, but the thing that people see through all of these hats and titles is her spirit of servanthood and love of her family. Amy's passion is to show women how they can stay home, raise their kids, and run a successful home business with their family. It is possible to have it all; she is living proof.

This family dynamic approach has earned them much recognition and multiple advancements. Amy also retired from her longtime corporate career at the age of 40 to raise her children and focus more on Wayside Gems.

Amy resides in Shelbyville, TN with her husband, Benji and their 4 children: Frank, Clara, Sam, and Nora. Together, they work their family business. They are members of Fair Haven Baptist Church and serve in several areas of ministry. Amy also volunteers at her children's school, assisting in math and reading fluency as well as Running Club. She is also serving on the Board of Directors for Church Girl CEO and is a 20+ year member of the Order of the Eastern Star. For fun, the family likes to help out on their multi-generational century farm, camping, dancing, and anything with Scouting BSA.

Born and raised in the suburbs of Chicago, Amy graduated from James B. Conant High School. She later earned her degree in math and science from Grand Valley State University in Allendale, MI.

Connect with Amy Philpott:

Website: waysidegems.com

Facebook: facebook.com/thewaysidegems
facebook.com/WaysideGemsVIP

Instagram: waysidegems

Email: thewaysidegems@gmail.com

Juggling the Chaos of Life
By Tracy Shorter

She was described as a pillar of strength, wisdom, dependability and loving in her own not-so-gooey way. Yet, she now found herself crying, kicking, and screaming on the floor with thoughts of never getting up.

How did she find herself at this point? She was not the one who behaved this way, even when she wanted to scream. She didn't have time for that! Solutions are what she produced, even when she wanted to run away. Suddenly, as she lay there on the floor, an ever-so-soft voice reminded her that she was built to handle the chaos in her life. Not only was she a Chaos Coordinator, but she also had an uncanny ability to calm the environment around her, even in the midst of chaos.

The situation described above is a true moment in time for my life. As I reflected on those ever-so-soft words, the term that stuck was Chaos Coordinator. I remember thinking, *who wants to go through life dealing with their own or other people's chaos?* Then, a quick reminder came that life will indeed bring you lemons, but you must determine how to make lemonade. Making lemonade sounds like a simple process, but to get the perfect batch of lemonade requires the correct balance of sour and sweet and the right amount of ice ☺.

But let's talk more about what a Chaos Coordinator does and the positive and negative vibes this superpower creates. According to the Urban Dictionary, a Chaos Coordinator *is a worker who keeps the company going by leading, organizing, planning, and delivering with a smile fueled by passion and caffeine, referred to as an excellent problem solver or able to juggle an insane number of activities at any given moment successfully.* I can identify with two of the above attributes, and while coordinating is not something I set out to do, I have consistently found myself in this position.

For as long as I can remember, my desire has been to help and serve others. In retrospect, I don't think I ever had a choice in the matter of service. My grandmother, Julia, whom we affectionately referred to as MaDear, started this for our family. Looking back, my grandmother had a business, not in the traditional sense of what we see today, but it was one she passed down to my mom and in turn, was passed down to me. It was the family business of community service, where she served in the community, her local church, and most importantly, her family. My very first remembrance of her community service was those Eastern Star meetings she attended. As she got dressed in that white dress and gloves, I always wanted to duplicate her and what she did. Looking back at my MaDear and Mom's involvement with community service, I saw firsthand that one person can make a difference. Sometimes the impact is small and immediate and other times you may not see it harvest. I think that when a person starts a business or new venture, one of the first people to get involved is the family members. But not everyone is meant to work in the family business as some skills can be taught while others are just naturally a part of you and ultimately become your purpose.

My grandmother first introduced my mom, who then introduced me to my first job in the family business. It was with a non-profit organization called The Help One Another Club, Inc., founded by Mrs. Geraldine Moore. This organization served the community by providing food boxes to seniors and families, free and discounted clothing, job assistance, school supplies, and backpacks for kids returning to school and more. At 15, I remember a food drive, where we gave out over 100 boxes of food and clothing. The event was a success and very chaotic, but I remember talking with Mrs.

Moore about how we could make it better by creating stations and only having a certain number of people in the building at one time.

For the next drive, we implemented a four-station rotation, and service was better for participants and volunteers. As I managed the door flow the day of the event, I was so excited to see my idea work and the impact it made for the people seeking help -- priceless for a young teenager.

When I got married and started my own family, my husband and I made the decision that my focus would be to just care for the family, so their chaos became my new priority. As a new wife and mother, I continued to be asked to plan trips, events, and assist people with life goals. I often wondered why and then when I was asked to serve in a leadership position at my church, I said yes for two reasons -- the opportunity to really see if I was really meant to do it and secondly, my pastor said they needed my help. I knew the church was a place known to traditionally help others, and I was at a point of desperately seeking my place. There is a scripture in Jeremiah 29:11, that says... *I know the plans I have for you saith the Lord, plan of good and not evil, plans to prosper and not harm.* I read this and if God was the one who has the plan for me, then I needed to connect with him to get it.

While serving as a leader in my church and other organizations has been a rewarding part of my life, one thing I have always wanted was my own business. I tried many things until I found my love for travel and the travel business. Some of the clients I serve know exactly what they want in creating their travel vacations or adventures. Then there are some who need to get away and have no idea where to start or they are trying to create travel plans for multi-generations which comes with its own challenges. It's true that too much of everyday life can get chaotic and my role in the lives of those faced with this situation is to be that advocate of support to help them organize between their possible and impossible. One thing I know is true. Like the serenity prayer, knowing the difference is your key to peace and eventual happiness. While I don't believe in impossibility, I do believe that when I do the possible, my partnership with God allows the impossible to become possible.

My time serving others in and out of ministry has allowed me to deepen my relationship with God, but it has also made me re-examine my role in the family business. For over the last 20 years, I have served my family, church, community, and travel clients, and not always in the correct order. It hasn't been until recently that I realized that we all must create healthy boundaries for ourselves. There is some chaos *we are not meant to coordinate.* Those particular people are thrust in the middle of the discourse, and they play a huge role in what is going on and sometimes the chaos they bring into our lives is just between them and God. As a coordinator, it's important to understand when you have to draw a line in the sand. You have to know when you are crossing boundaries and if your involvement will disrupt your peace or have a negative impact on your life.

In other words, it's not your fight.

You see, sometimes the coordinator wants it more than the person they are assisting. When this happens and full participation is not given, you can overstep and take on the responsibility yourself, risk pushing your agenda too hard, and completely discourage the person you are assisting. As a coordinator, when I have moved past that line, I have found myself lacking movement and becoming frustrated at the person I was set to serve, spinning my wheels.

This superpower can have a powerful impact and to successfully serve in it, you must understand that the people you serve have a part to play in their own success. Your role as Chaos Coordinator is to come into the situation temporarily to be a guide, a cheerleader, or maybe a visionary when needed, but most importantly, it is to direct them back with a step-by-step blueprint toward a life of peace and joy, but they make the steps. In order to minimize crossing boundaries when helping others, here are three (3) things to remember:

1. Create a ritual to reset: When life gets stressful, and you are juggling a lot of things, it is important to reset. Failure to reset creates an opportunity to make mistakes or damage relationships due to your grouchy nature of not taking the time to do self-care. ☺.

2. Learn the art of saying NO!: Saying yes to activities because we feel obligated often happens with family and friends or the need to just be busy. But like eating too much candy can make you sick, being busy with tasks you are not meant to do can have the same effect. Coordinators are to make an impact for those they are assigned to but that assignment does not extend to everyone we meet.

3. Find your support person: While you are the support person for the people you are assisting, don't leave yourself out. Everybody needs a cheerleader, a counselor, and a safe place to share feelings or challenges. While your gift allows you the opportunity to make others' lives easier, without being able to refill your cup that is consistently pouring out, your well will eventually dry up.

Finally, while the rewards are great, the challenges have their effect too. My last recommendation is this: When you give yourself the absolute best first, you are then able to give others the absolute best because you recognize what it looks like.

Take care my fellow coordinators and know I am always cheering for YOU!

Reflection/Notes

What are your key takeaways?

Were there any surprising moments that spoke to your soul?

What would you share with others?

What superpowers aligned with yours?

About Tracy D. Shorter

Whenever you interact with Tracy Shorter, you will leave encouraged, supported, and have a new cheerleader on this journey we call LIFE! With a strong servant's heart and over 15 years of strategic planning experience, she has been helping others fulfill their vision and create memories through weddings, special events and her non-profit work under *Tracy Shorter Enterprises.*

In 2016, the Lord spoke the word **BELIEVE** to Tracy and unbeknownst to her, she would need it more than ever, because in 2018 as life did a shift, an unexpected health forecast came without warning. After months of prayer, the message to that one simple word BELIEVE was not just for Tracy, but it was clear that she was to spread that message to those around her. Using 7 principles from the word BELIEVE, a new purpose unfolded to help others uncover their purpose and develop a plan to walk and live it every day!

With her 15-plus years' experience as a former wedding/event planner, Tracy has a broad knowledge in planning group and individual travel through her travel agency, *Shorter Route Travel.* She has been in the travel industry since 2017, and as a Group and Cruise Travel Specialist, providing her clients with excellent customer service is her top priority. A few of her personal and group travel destinations have included *Jamaica, Puerto Rico, San Cabo, St. Thomas, Nassau, and Alaska.*

Tracy is a published author and motivational speaker. Her books include:

Believe and Rediscover: A 31-day Journal to Self-Discovery, two (2) collaboratives:

SheCeo and Truth. Tracy's story is powerful and could speak to the lives of many.

She is available to speak on a number of topics such as The B.E.L.I.E.V.E Framework, Building your Circle of Influence, and How Travel Adventures Will Enrich your Life, just to name a few.

Tracy is married to her high school sweetheart, Rolando and they have 2 children, Jasmine and Christian. As an active member in her church, Revelation Knowledge Bible Church, she serves as the Financial Director, Deaconess and a member of the Special Events Committee.

Connect with Tracy Shorter

Email: tracy@shorterenterprises.net

Facebook: www.facebook.com/shorterroutetravel

Private Travel Group:

www.facebook.com/AdventureswithShorterRouteTravel

WRITE THAT THANG DOWN!
By JC Gardner

There is something special and unique about the written word.

When you are speaking with someone, you can see facial expressions and body language. You can tell if they are interested in what you are saying or not paying attention. If you are in front of an audience speaking, you can feel if the audience is giving you high energy, chatting during your presentation, or falling asleep. Public speaking is a skill. Some have it naturally and some have to work at it. It can wreck your nerves and no matter how rehearsed you are, getting up in front of that crowd can make you forget your five-star presentation. Looking out into the sea of "strangers" can make the most confident person uncomfortable and instead of owning the audience, they end up owning you!

Have you ever wanted to tell someone to their face that you are angry with them? You sit in your car and rehearse that fired-up speech and you are really going to give it to them so they can feel the depth of your anguish. Yet when it's time, your heart is palpitating, palms are sweaty, and when you open your mouth, all of that venom just dissipates. It doesn't even come out the way you want it to.

And the opposite can happen too. Not only did you say everything you rehearsed, you went overboard and said some things you can never take back. Your lips betrayed you and as Marcus Garvey noted: "The pen is mightier than the sword, but the tongue is mightier than them both put together." You threw verbal daggers at the heart and possibly burnt the bridge of forgiveness.

How about gathering the courage to say those three heartfelt words: **I love you**. Will it be reciprocated when you say it? Will he/she feel the same way? There is joy in your soul, and you've been building up the courage to express your feelings, but you can't get it together. Doubt creeps in about verbally sharing these deep emotions and you just let it go.

In each of these scenarios, having your thoughts in writing is invaluable, even for the public speaker, which takes time, energy, and a good bit of confidence. Some people say memorizing your remarks shows professionalism; I say having your presentation on the podium with you shows realism. It actually can be your saving grace having it there to glance at every now and then, or it may even ground you and help you remember what it is you want to say. Instead of looking out into the crowd, you can focus on that podium until you get more comfortable with eye contact with strangers in the audience. The point is that without it being in writing, you are indeed relying on memory. Nothing wrong with that but what if for some reason you fall ill or can't make the event? Your "presence" can still be felt because you took the time to put it all in writing, and someone you trust can still present the written word on your behalf.

Another value to having it in writing is that it can easily be repurposed for different audiences and different seasons. No reinventing the wheel – just swapping out a few spokes!

Let's take the angry situation. If I had a hundred dollars for every angry email or letter I wrote that *did not get sent*, I'd be a millionaire. The beautiful thing about writing it down first is that it allows you to express yourself and include all of your real thoughts -- good, bad, or indifferent. The paper (journal, notebook, keyboard) can harbor all of your deepest, darkest secrets and it will never forsake you or tell a soul unless you choose to release it. I'm not ashamed to admit that there were days I almost thought my keyboard was going to crack in half because I was hammering out my fury about something I was upset about. I mean that keyboard was capturing exactly what I wanted to say. When we are angry, a lot of times our emotions are out of control and out of character. We don't even take time to pray, and we let the flesh have its way. It's all reactionary. We may say, "Jesus take the wheel," but those words have no meaning, as we would be using our own GPS and have our foot on the gas, telling Him how to drive.

I believe there is a spirituality to the art of writing. It can cleanse your mind of all that clutter and allow you to release your innermost thoughts without repercussion or retribution. Taking the time to write down what is bothering you can save you a lot of heartache and quite frankly, embarrassment. No, you will not always have this luxury, but when you do, try it and see if you still want to bum-rush the person who hurt you. I'm betting that your approach will change when you force yourself to reflect on how your words would make them feel.

Telling stories or other literary visions through the power of the pen is my superpower. Seeing narratives come to life through the written word is where I thrive. I've had this gift for many years, since the age of 12. What started out as a way to just pass the time turned into my passion. My writing was stifled due to an unfortunate event in my youth, where a teacher humiliated me in class. There is a lot more to it but what happened that fateful days caused me to squander my gift for many years, although the writing never stopped because what God has planted inside of you no [wo]man can destroy. You may try to run away from it or even suppress it, but whatever story you have inside of you is there for a reason.

It's there to not only help you, but it's there to help someone else know they can make it because you did; they can start a business because you showed them how; they can survive trauma because you persevered through the storm.

There is no doubt my superpower is from the Creator, and once he set me free, it was my mandate to help others do the same thing.

Everyone is not a writer though. They rather channel their creativity into math and science; or the thought of making the time to sit and write doesn't exactly bring them joy...yet they still have something to share. That is where ghostwriting comes in.

A ghostwriter is almost always a paid service where a skilled writer works closely with you to tell your story. They write the book for you and at the end, you receive the manuscript to market fully as your own. So even if you do not like to write, there is a way to get your story (presentation, booklet) in print.

Ghostwriting is something I enjoy but it can drain your soul. I *become* the client so that the book reads as if the client wrote it, which takes time, energy, and dedication on both parts. It has been a blessing for me to help many people through this process, however, depending on what their story is, I have to take a lot of mental breaks so I can refuel and be fully present for our sessions.

I also love fiction writing. That allows me to venture into "fantasy" territory and become other people for a time. Some ask, "Where do I get the characters that I write about?" They just show up. Yes, they show up in my car, in the grocery store, during my walks, and in my dreams. They come to me, and I've always been like that.

When they show up, I literally see them – all their hopes and desires come with them too. Even when I write poems, songs, essays, etc., 99% of the time it is my creativity on overdrive, and I can't stop it.

Enough about me. Let's focus on how you can use the stroke of a pen in ways that enhance your life today or how you can start improving/nurturing your writing journey. Here are some pointers that may relate to you.

1. **Writing is such a chore!** If this is you but you know you are required to write, whether for work or school, just take it one day at a time and practice using writing prompts to get your creativity flowing such as:

   a. The best/worst thing about today was XXXX and this is why.

   b. In three years, I hope I am doing/owning/driving XXXX.

   c. My dream getaway is XXXX and the reason why.

It's that simple! The point is to write in increments until it gets comfortable.

The best part is that this is for you, so all typos are between you and Jesus 😊 For your work or school requirements, the best thing to do is start early! Do not try to cram it in the night before it's due and get all stressed out. This will take a bit of planning, but it will be worth it in the end.

❖ **Your A-ha Moment:** Do you know you can record your remarks and then have it transcribed through an online service? I know this just set someone free!

2.   **So many stories, so little time!** If you know you have a story to share and there are many different topics and themes, write them ALL down then decide: Are they books or are they articles? Every story is not a book. Once you do that discernment, lean into the one you know the most about. That way, all of the details should be at your fingertips and not a chore.

   ❖   **Your A-ha Moment**: Make an outline of all of the chapters for your book or all of the points you want to make. This will help you get clarity.

3.   **I can't express my true feelings to people; the words are stuck!** Well, you may be surprised by this response, but that's why there are hundreds of greeting cards! Yes, greetings cards are expressions of the written word. I spend a lot of time picking out greeting cards because I'm serious about what I'm "saying" to people, and I want it to fit the moment. There is nothing wrong with using other written media to express your thoughts.

   ❖ **Your A-ha Moment**: Remember earlier I referenced people having trouble saying, "I love you?" Greeting cards would be ideal and not only that, skilled writers also can do personalized poems just for you using your thoughts.

4. **I start writing then go off track**. This is where a writing coach can help you stay focused, but also earlier, I mentioned having an outline (see A-ha

Moment in #1). That should keep you focused.

As you can see, writing can take on all shapes and forms – from poetry to articles, brochures, pamphlets – the list is endless. Side note: Do you know that it is estimated that 4 million book titles are published each year?[1] Talk about the power of the pen! That just shows you that the written word remains one of the best ways to get your point across, whether personal, professional, or even as a hobby. It has global outreach and what you have to share is not always just for you but can be a blessing to others.

---

[1] https://www.tonerbuzz.com/blog/how-many-books-are-published-each-year/

Reflection/Notes

What are your key takeaways?

Were there any surprising moments that spoke to your soul?

What would you share with others?

What superpowers aligned with yours?

About JC Gardner

JC Gardner is an international, award-winning author, speaker, poet, writing coach, and ghostwriter. Helping authors bring their projects to life through her coaching program is a blessing and a gift. She has written and coauthored numerous books, along with contributing to many publications. Her novel, "Heated," is an urban dramedy about a single mother's plight to do better despite her negative circumstances. It is the recipient of an IPPY Award, a Distinguished Author's Guild Award, and an Amazon bestseller. JC is also a contributor and Senior Editor for Church Girl CEO Magazine and a writing coach and mentor as part of the Youth Writer's Rock nonprofit organization. In 2023, JC was nominated for Editor of the Year by I.AM.Her International.

JC was a closet writer for many years due to a devastating blow in her past that silenced her creativity and almost derailed her God-given talent of being an entertainer and storyteller through the written word. After a phenomenal, spiritual breakthrough, it was clear that what God has placed in your heart, no one can take away. She is a natural-born writer; it is infused in her D.N.A. and believes everyone's D.N.A. makes them **D**eliberately **N**ot **A**verage!

By day, JC is a National Advisor at an international nonprofit. By candlelight, she writes! She has been married for over 36 years and has two successful grown children.

Connect With JC Gardner:

Facebook: https://www.facebook.com/AuthorJCG

Instagram: https://www.instagram.com/author_jcg/

Websites: www.blossomlitservices.com / www.jc-gardner.com

Email: jc@blossomlitservices.com

GIRL, STAY FOCUSED
By Braidley Ayuma

Focus is one thing that drives success in all spheres of life. I have maintained focus from an early stage of my life for a number of reasons. In essence, I had no choice but to focus on the little things I had to do in order to be successful in life. From my background view, my parents made a lot of sacrifices with the little they had to make sure that we made it through school. I made a promise from an early stage that I would do what it takes to ensure that all their efforts would not be in vain. I would do what it takes to ensure that they are fully compensated for the love, attention, affection, efforts, and finances they had given to ensure that we would make it in life.

Maintaining focus made me avoid distractions that would deter the main course of action. The trajectory of my success would not allow certain aspects of life that would make it difficult to maintain the main course of action. For instance, I had to deal with a lot of challenges from peers, especially during my teenage stages of life. It was not easy as most of my peers came from families that were financially stable and well-established. The worst was trying to maintain a status quo that could not be easily maintained. With focus, I was able to accept my situation regardless of the bullying and mockery that came from classmates who felt they were in a better position in life. I look back and appreciate what I have been able to achieve at the moment. Regardless of the temptations that come with peer pressure, I maintained clear focus and always kept my eye on the goal.

To date, I believe that focus is key not only in school, but also in other areas of life. You need to focus even at work to ensure your best results have been achieved. With better results, attaining the necessary professional growth in the workplace would be easy. As I aim to grow a professional path working with phenomenal women leaders in USA, I will always look back and thank my determination and the little girl in me for staying focused. It made me maintain the trajectory of success without looking sideways on aspects that would derail me in any way. As an upcoming mentor, I will always advise young people who are going through the same to always focus and remain objective on the simple issues that would lead them to success. Focus gives us the opportunity to connect the simple dots of success and build a strong foundation to avoid a reverse gear that would draw you back to a life of misery. I wake up every single day with the intention of changing my life and that of my parents who have sacrificed a lot to get me to where I am today.

I have fought against all odds to get to get to this current status. This is what I call *pure determination*. As indicated earlier, my parents did their best with the little they had to take me to the best schools possible. This means that I schooled with rich kids who had everything they wanted in life. While at times I had to walk to school. This really hurt but pushed me to work extra hard to ensure I could give my kids the very best in life. It took an extra kind of determination to ensure that I could learn and achieve in this kind of imbalanced social environment. With a lot of criticism all around, I worked to ensure that I would become the best at what I do. Staying focused in my class was a way of showing my peers that I could set standards regardless of my low economic status. It was the only way I could equalize the odds to show them that status was not a thing that defined who we were. I worked extremely hard to outdo the challenges I faced in almost area and make a name in an environment that was extremely challenging. I use the same arsenal of determination to fight any odds that would come along this journey of success. There is a high level of competition among people who seeking the same opportunity to work as Virtual Assistants, and it is not easy to stand out in a sea of qualified candidates. In this case, I always need to work extra hard to ensure that a unique brand image has been created. In turn, this would work to ensure that I gain and sustain a competitive edge over everyone else. My self-esteem is one arsenal tool that makes me fight against this kind of competition regardless of how good the other people are that come on board. If I did it in the past during my schooling stages to get to where I am today, I would use the same technique to fight all the way to the end. As I make use of this determination, I do not at any point underrate the many other people who are on board. I learn from the best in the industry, and I am always open to advice and filter out what is not working. This is exactly what I

used to do growing up in extreme poverty. With this, I maintain an advantage over many other scholars and attract a following that would take me from one position to another. With the little my parents had, they made sure we could get something. if not everything, and at least the tuition fee was paid. I believe that everything that happened along this journey of success did not take place by chance.

Over the years, I have come to learn humility is a key aspect in the development of any career path. From my background, I came to learn that my parents did a great job in shaping my character as far as humility is concerned. My parents always insisted on respecting the aspects of protocol from all angles. With this in mind, I have grown up respecting people regardless of whether they are older or younger than me. The same would also apply to my engagement in any professional organizational setting. With proper structures put in place, I have learned that there will be someone above and below my rank. With humility, I am able to respect all the protocols of engagement at work. This trait has offered me the opportunity to always learn from all angles and grow my knowledge in an all-around manner. Everyone in the world has a purpose and if proper engagement is done, I will take advantage of it and add to new ways to build up my skills. With a focus on growing a professional career in the virtual world, my goal is to be as humble as possible in order to accommodate everyone that comes my way. In the end, I believe that this will offer me an opportunity to promote my teamwork spirit and always work to produce better results. I learn to always remain accountable on all operations that I handle on a daily basis without compromising the final result.

Education institutions play an influential role in shaping professional careers and skill sets; however, I hold a personal belief that there is a lot to learn from people who have a diverse perspective. At the end of the day, this kind of knowledge will only be noise from people if one is not humble enough to listen to what another person is saying and try to apply what works for them. Literally, we all come from different background settings and react and respond to issues in different ways. With such a diverse world, a lot of knowledge can be drawn from people and applied in different ways in order to gain success.

As I develop through the different stages of life, I take any opportunity to absorb knowledge from all angles with the highest level of humility possible. At the end of the day, I believe that not every person that offers their view may be accurate. But it is upon me to discern what has been discussed and decide on what to apply to both my career and personal life as well. As I continue building my business and advancing as a professional Virtual Assistant, this is the best strategy that I will employ from time to time until I cement a legacy that will have a positive impact in society and for my kids. From my past experience, I am on a journey that will have a positive impact on the people I will be working with and any other person that has made a positive contribution to what I am today.

As a woman, I applaud all other women who are making an effort to grow and make a positive impact in society. The odds are stacked against us and in order to achieve, one must stand out and fight extremely hard. I am a young woman who is striving to encourage and influence many other women across the world. Part of my need and thirst to work with women from abroad and be successful is so that young women from where I come from can read between the lines and understand that indeed, there is hope at the end of the tunnel. With focus, faith, determination, and consistency, the world will gradually come to terms that women have a greater position in society. Through my testimony, I believe the world will see the need to increase the number of women in leadership and management positions. I fight this goal with the belief that many other women will come along to encourage one another and remain consistent on the trajectory of success. I believe that this course I have taken will bring on board many changes that are desired by many silent women who are suffering without the world noticing.

The long race is finally supported by the will of God. As a Christian, I have always held faith as one of the driving factors in my path of success. God has brought me a long way and would not abandon me after all that I have gone through. Every morning I wake up and pray that even though times are hard, the Lord Almighty should keep my head up to manage all other challenges that I would meet along the way. Giving up is not an option, thus, all potential women should come on board to support the common course of one girls who have suffered for a very long time. Part of my desire is to ensure that I become a visible influencer to members of my society and the entire world. With the onset of technology, I will always do what it takes to make a lasting impact for the coming generations to see and appreciate. My family is my world; my little precious son and daughter give me a reason to wake up every day and keep going. My husband is my absolute support system and my friend. I love my extended community of friends and family that see me through my happy and sad moments. For my parents, I will always do what it takes to make you proud and happy. I might not give you the entire world at the moment, however, time will come when you'll realize that I was not born by chance and every little deed that you have initiated will not go in vain. The same applies to my siblings and any other person that has ensured that the path I have taken is a success.

We have all struggled to make it through and such effort will never go in vain. As I look toward what life has to offer in future, I urge everyone to always remain focused on their goals and have someone in your corner whenever you feel you need someone close to talk to.

It is the only route to make us win and reclaim our glory once again.

Reflection/Notes

What are your key takeaways?

Were there any surprising moments that spoke to your soul?

What would you share with others?

What superpowers aligned with yours?

About Braidley Ayuma

Braidley Ayuma, an Executive Assistant and Social Media Manager, is the CEO and Founder of **Sisters From Kenya**. As the CEO, Braidley manages a team of virtual assistants that help busy, high-end women entrepreneurs maximize their time, allowing them to focus on more important issues in their lives and businesses.

As a management specialist, her team of virtual assistants are top-notch, serving clients globally by lending their expertise in Project Management, Customer Service, and Event Planning, and much more! They live out their core values of communication, commitment, integrity, excellence, passion, and balance in everything they do, ensuring the client's needs are met with exceptional service.

Braidley has over four years of experience and has received accolades from various companies she has supported. She is also a dedicated mother and wife and enjoys spending time with her family.

If you are in need of a virtual assistant, connect with Braidley to see how she can help you shine.

Connect with Braidley:

Website: http://sistersfromkenya.com/

Email: braidkimber@gmail.com
/sistersfromkenya@gmail.com,

Phone: +254726725977

At Deborah Franklin Publishing (DFP), we pride ourselves on being a full-service publishing house that is large enough to serve you, yet small enough to need you. We believe in providing personalized attention to all our clients, recognizing that each author and their book have unique goals and aspirations.

From the very beginning, we are here to assist you every step of the way, from the inception of your book idea to the final stages of publishing and launching. Our dedicated team of award-winning editors and designers will work closely with you, ensuring that your vision is brought to life and that your manuscript reaches its full potential.

Our editors are not only experienced but have also been recognized for their excellence in the industry. They will meticulously review your manuscript, providing insightful feedback, and ensuring that your writing is refined and polished. Our designers, on the other hand, will collaborate with you to create captivating cover designs and interior layouts that will catch the eye of your target audience.

At DFP, we understand that publishing a book is just the first step. That's why we go beyond traditional publishing services. We act as your personal concierge for all your publishing and marketing needs. Whether it's strategizing your book launch, implementing effective marketing campaigns, or exploring distribution options, we are here to guide and support you throughout the entire process.

Your success is our priority, and we are dedicated to being by your side as you embark on your publishing journey. With our expertise and commitment, we strive to be the catalyst for your accomplishments as an author.

We look forward to working with you and helping you achieve your publishing goals.

Betty Jean's food hut was established June 9,2018 by Owner Paulette Bice who named it after her late mother Betty Jean Bice.

Our company specializes in authentic grilled food. We offer catering, on-site grilling for all events including sports.

Contact us today for your special events. Paulette Bice 2055679168 bjfoodhut@gmail.com

Nathalie Loma Bridal

Wedding Dresses, Tuxedo/Suits & Accessories

520 N. Michigan Ave. Chicago IL
Info@nathalieloma.com (312) 285 - 2128
Nathalieloma.com

95

RIGHT FINANCIAL SOLUTIONS

Lifetime cover for a Lifetime of protection

- LIFE INSURANCE
- LONG TERM CARE
- RETIREMENT PLANNING
- INVESTMENT
- FINAL EXPENSE
- TAX SAVING STRATEGIES

MIREILLE AGONZAN
FINANCIAL PROFESSIONAL

☎ +1 (323)-667-5226   📍 Mireille Agonzan   ✉ Mireille@rightfinanciasolutions.com

PUBLISHING

THE CONCIERGE OF PUBLISHING

www.ingramcontent.com/pod-product-compliance
Lightning Source LLC
Chambersburg PA
CBHW060336130626
46553CB00003B/1021